SHIT

PISS

STRESS

ASTOR QUINTANA

WRITERS REPUBLIC L.L.C.
515 Summit Ave. Unit R1
Union City, NJ 07087, USA

Website: *www.writersrepublic.com*
Hotline: *1-877-656-6838*
Email: *info@writersrepublic.com*

Ordering Information:
Quantity sales. Special discounts are available on quantity purchases by corporations, associations, and others. For details, contact the publisher at the address above.

Library of Congress Control Number: 2021912444
ISBN-13:   978-1-63728-662-3 [Paperback Edition]
                    978-1-63728-671-5 [Hardback Edition]
                    978-1-63728-663-0 [Digital Edition]

Rev. date: 06/17/2021

Acknowledgment

To my parents, the two people who are
tougher than life itself, and loved us
more than they loved themselves.

INTRODUCTION

Stress is a build up; it grows and spreads inside of you until it eats you up. Just like shit, piss, toxins, excess of anything, it all needs to be released, thrown away, evacuated. Easy to say, I know, but I will try to give you practical, no bullshit tips to get rid of stress. I am a psychologist; therefore I know the science of it. But I am also a man, a husband, a father, a store manager that deals with a lot of crap daily and needs to have a balance so I don't bite anyone's head off, and don't go crazy. Like any other human being, we all deal with issues on a daily basis.

How many books have been written about this matter, and right after you read it, you end up more stressed with the added activities the book suggests to fight stress? Give me a break, will ya. My intention is to redirect your attention, not add bullshit nor will I suggest taking away. I am sure this will change your mindset.

No, I did not make a long, boring ass study to show you stats, I do have relatable situations where I can prove that these work. I might throw in some support material to back up what I am saying, mostly from experience. These just to show, prove, how these points, attitudes have genuinely changed me and others and taken to higher levels of physical wellness, mental sanity, and spiritual wholeness.

So, give me a bit of your time, I will not take much of it since it is precious, I promise you will laugh a bit too, which helps as well, and in time it will save you.

Since I will say it as it is, I will be cussing, so beware if you are sensitive to profanity, which I do not care. I will be as honest as I can.

SEX

Oh yeah!!! Sex, dirty, wild, wet, nasty sex. Completely underrated and taken for granted by the ones who have easy access to it. Thrown away to the dark corner of the room like an old dirty sock. We want sex, we fucking need sex. It has been vulgarized, I cannot deny that, and has set ridiculous standards to good sex. I am talking about porn, which only proves that it is a great thing. Unfortunately, many couples look elsewhere for this yummy, delightful treat. Naughty, naughty!!

But here is the deal, bonds are been broken at our homes, therefore attraction goes out the door. So we need to connect with each other more than we connect to the social media world. Face it, lift up your dumbass face from the phone, and take a look at your sexy wife walking around the house in her panties and that old shirt, braless, showered; tell me it doesn't turn you on.

Anyway, sex is the best stress releasing activity by far. The whole kissing, caressing, grabbing, sweating, shoving, staring, involves every drop of your existence.

The only con about sex is that it is not always available for many reasons, your SO (significant other) is sick, menstruation, away on a trip, mad, and many other reasons. But, always try to make time for this, it is worth it, and sex is not only the act; it starts from that morning smack on the ass and the grunt. The "you look hot" and a nice kiss before they go to work. When you get home, you will get it.

Besides from being the best feeling in the world, it is beneficial for your overall health, and this is why:

1. Makes you feel good, due to the release of dopamine (a neurotransmitter that activates the reward center of the brain)
2. Acts as an antidepressant, making us feel better about ourselves, we can all agree that is an all-around awesome feeling. Who has sex and feels shitty afterwards?
3. Relieves pain (how good is that?). This is a sucker punch to those who use "I have a headache" as an excuse to NOT have sex that day, well here is your Valium, baby. Start looking for other excuses.
4. Calms you down by lowering your blood pressure, making you have better responses to stressful situations. A good tip for whenever you have meetings the next day or have morning quickie. Just saying.
5. Helps you sleep better, yes, it helps you sleep better, restful sleep, replenishing sleep with a big ass smile on your face.

Now pay attention to this next point. I do not promote promiscuity, nor am I implying you go on a sex spree every time you want sex. I promote faithfulness; sex with the one you love is perfect.

If true stress release is desired from this precious gift, it is to be shared with the one you love.

Admit it, sex with an attractive person you just met is good, you reach orgasm and enjoy it, but sex with that one person you love, you reach heaven.

So you see, this is not an activity, homework, or hobby I am adding to your daily routine. This is something you have been doing for a while, but kind of forgot how good it feels. I cannot tell you how to spice it up. That is your problem, I am a psychologist and there are many ways people enjoy this, whatever rocks your world, baby. But do it, enjoy it, go crazy, and live it. The best way to spice it up is being honest with each other and open up to what you want to do.

Don't take your partner for granted. I know lots of couples that lose interest in each other, you are only bringing more problems, more stress. There is always something that tie you up for good times. Don't let that go, and the physical level can always make your mind blow. I know this by experience. Try having sex after having a discussion, you'll end up moaning "I'm sorry, I love you, Oh God", it comes out naturally. And that is raw, it is a naked confession that puts you out there with the one you love.

EXERCISE

This activity is available all the time. Exercise helps us in every damn way possible. Not only is it an enormous help to get rid of stress, but it also keeps you in good shape and healthy, this helping boost your self-esteem and confidence.

I will not lie to you, not always will you want to do it, some days you will feel tired and exhausted, but I can guarantee that if you push your self to do it even though you are tired, you will definitely feel much better by the end of your workout. You will not regret shaking off the exhaustion and pushing yourself to do some exercise. I know this by experience.

I am a husband, father, I work in a store, I barely have time, but I have the desire to feel better, look better, plus, I am motivated to get into the TV business, so I have to stay in shape. I am not talking smack, let me prove to you that time is in your hands, and you have it at your disposal, just got to be persistent enough. This is my daily story:

I wake up every day at 5:30 am, shower, get dressed, wake up my children, dress them up, cook breakfast for them, take them to school, I am at work by 9 am. I manage a fishing store, I send orders out, receive the product, clean up, assist walk-in customers. By 5 pm, I leave to pick up my beautiful children, go home, shower them, make dinner, we have dinner together, watch a little TV, play, by 7:30 they are laying down and getting ready to sleep. Both of my kids have a bond with me that is unexplainable. They love to go to sleep with me by their side, no matter if I stay there silent. So, I take turns with each, since they both have their own rooms. So I am out of their rooms by around 8:45 pm, I get ready for the gym, hit the gym until 9:45 or so, come back home, help my wife with cleaning or whatever, spend some time with her, talk, eat, laugh, watch a movie, do something nasty, whatever. So I go to bed at around 11 pm. So yes, I am a normal human being, and we all have time to exercise, it will only benefit you if you do it.

You don't need to go to a fancy gym or have all the equipment in the world. It can be any kind, there are thousands of exercises you can do, if you don't have money for the gym, no need to, you have the floor of your living room, do some push-ups, crunches, burpees, squats. I go to a gym because is part of the rental community, if that wasn't there, I'd be home killing it in the living room.

Not one specific exercise is better for you than the rest. Just go with the one you enjoy the most doing, and that is it. It can be jogging, swimming, cycling, hiking, yoga, any sport that requires having a team, weight lifting, boxing, whatever goes with your liking.

My personal preference is an intense workout, grinding, and full body challenge. I am old school, I like boxing, slamming a big ass tire with a 12lb sledgehammer, I love bodyweight lifting, I have tried all this new CrossFit, which is awesome. These are my personal favorites, they bring out the best in me, and they challenge my body and mind. No matter how tired I am, these exercises demand mental assurance that you can do it, obliging the body to go further. So you set new limits to yourself, you focus on an activity that you will be triumphant. And this is an effective and tough stress-relieving activity that will help you every day.

Stress is the body's way of responding to danger or demands. This means that during stress, your body aches, some parts more than others. Exercise is your "pill" to take away that pain. You may wonder how.

- Well, apart from loosening and strengthening your muscles, it pumps more blood to your brain, oxygenating it more, improving your neuronal activity.
- It pumps up your endorphins (these are your feel-good neurotransmitters)
- Improves your sleep
- Improves your self-confidence
- It is a form of meditation

Meditation? Really? I thought meditation was closing your eyes, deep breathing, incenses, connecting with the universe and all that. But here is how you compare exercise to a form of meditation: you are letting go of daily irritations to focus on your exercise and obtaining a positive outcome. The difference is that this is a active meditation. You release negative vibes to bring in the positive, you focus on your movements, the right movements to be stronger, healthier, and at the end, you have a lighter mind and spirit. Nobody comes out of an exercise feeling like shit or dull, you might feel tiresome, but a good tired, lighter, and happier.

Many have a false image or idea that you have to exercise for hours. This is wrong, don't let anybody tell you this. Unless your profession is bodybuilding. But this is not directed at you, this is for the average Joe.

All you need is 20 to 30 minutes a day to workout and release some stress. If you want to really get into better results and quicker, change your fucking diet. Eat well, no secrets behind this, just remove all the shit you know you shouldn't be eating and that is it. You will feel the difference, and of course, less stress.

Now, the point of the exercise is to fight stress, doing something you enjoy doing to get a positive outcome. My biggest and strongest suggestion to you is do not stress over losing an enormous amount of pounds in a certain amount of time. This is unreal, unhealthy, and out of focus. Your focus should be feeling better, by feeling better you will look better. Enjoy the process, the results will show in time. I lost 30lbs in like 4 months, never weighed myself until I felt my clothes were feeling baggier and I needed to buy smaller pants. It was safe enough to go weigh in. The point is mental and physical health, not getting Hollywood body in 2 months.

NOT GIVING A FUCK

How beautiful it is to be carefree. We are drawn to care for everything all the time, everything that happens, that is said, done, every like or dislike. Countless people wake up, and the first thing they do is grab their phones and check how many people liked whatever they shared on any social media, how many people added them overnight, how many followers, comments. Let me ask you this: how will that change or better your day? Is it really important? I mean, unless you are running a business, but on a personal profile, on a personal level, does it really matter?

The objective, as I assume, of any social media is sharing moments, connecting with family and friends abroad, not a race or competition of likes, amount of followers.

This goes for everything in life, time is a measuring unit that cannot turn back around. So, either you spend time caring for whatever is worth caring for, or waste it stressing over bullshit that does not matter. Choose wisely, be smart when you use your time and energy.

Don't get me wrong, I care, I really do; I care about family, I care about my dreams, and that's about it. I care about being a good human being and teaching my children to be likewise. There are limits of caring, you can only do so much, give enough fucks, but when it affects your peace, your family life, when it obstructs your path to your self-realization, it's not healthy.

The rest of the world will not come to your rescue, nobody else cares if you have or don't have a million followers, or what you wear, what books you read. Sorry to burst your bubble there, pumpkin, but it is not easy. So why waste time trying to save the world? We can do so much by expressing love and care to the ones we love.

Here is the issue, when we care too much for every damn thing that surrounds us, we become bitter, we fight, we become toxic and conflictive. So, we waste time putting our attention, our focus, and our energy on things that don't really need it, on things that can get by on their own. Let loose, let go of those worries. Be more selective about what deserves your attention and energy.

Focus on you, and it sounds selfish, I know. But stressing over what the boss said, what she said, what others think will only drain you and consume you. Just do the best because you want to do your best without caring about what others say.

My father used to tell me, "Astor, Siempre hay un hijueputa", which translates to "Astor, there is always a son of a bitch"; meaning, you will always find an asshole that will try to fuck up your groove.

And let me tell you just how I got this attitude. I started working after my father died when I was 16 years old. When I was 24 or so, I used to work at a call center in Honduras. I made some friends and one of them whose name I will leave out was a good-hearted guy who worked really hard, stressed out over everything, trying to do great and make some brownie points with the bosses. One day he stopped coming to work, I heard he had pneumonia. I got sad, it sucked for a young guy to get sick like that; he used to smoke a lot as well. So it was not such a surprise either. Days later, I got the news he died. A young man, with a future ahead, died. A week after that, I come into my job, and on his cubicle, there was his substitute, just a new guy taking his place, the company was still running. This opened my eyes.

Another day, I was very sick, I used to get asthma attacks; I woke up feeling like shit, wheezing like a dying cat, and still getting ready to go work. My brother stopped me and told me to call in sick, "the company will not go bankrupt if you miss one day over your health, your health is more important". So I stayed, nothing happened, the day went by, I went the next day and everything was cool.

In another job, these guys used to work days in days out to get more money, and then I heard they also died. How ugly and terrifying it is to hear people around you dying, so young, knowing they will simply be replaced for the next in line, and knowing they spent so much time working hard and stressing.

So I chose to be more selective about what deserves my time, my energy, my attention, this helps me reduce my stress. One very good friend once told me, "If your problems have a solution, why worry? If they do not have a solution, why worry, bro?" This made me laugh at how accurate it is and simple.

So consider in making this part of your mantras, your attitude, and philosophy. It will save you from a lot of stupid stress.

WRITING
(or any craft)

There is always one craft we enjoy doing. Whether is writing (which is my case), painting, woodworking, pottery, sculpting, cooking, baking, or any other things that require your hands and mind, helps you release stress. It can be anything, putting your mind and hands to work divert your attention to something other than the daily routine. Crafts help you the following way:

- Diverts your focus from stress. Concentrating on a task you enjoy, an activity that is of your liking will make you put all your attention on completing it. Which brings me to the next point.
- Strengthens your confidence in your own abilities. Completing a task will boost confidence and self-esteem.
- Gives you mastership over something you have control. A craft is something you choose to do, out of passion and ability. Therefore, it will lead you to become savvy on the subject and learn new and better ways to do it, so it will take you to be a master of your craft.

- Broadens social horizons. A craft will take you to connect with people from different backgrounds and culture that share similar preferences.
- If performed with full consciousness it can become meditative. Just like exercise, focusing on an activity that requires concentration, hands-on work, completing a task, will become a positive meditative session.

In my case, I love writing (duuhhh!!!), additional to that, I enjoy cooking and baking, and these two are as enjoyable to me as writing. The whole process of it, from going to the store and visualizing what dish can be done with this and that ingredient, what elements go together and seeing the dish served and have not even paid yet.

Baking needs more of your focus than cooking. We are talking about exact measures; you cannot go over or under the measures of yeast, flour, sugar or any other element needed, depending on the bread you're baking.

No, I do not bake cakes or cupcakes, I hate it, but that's just me. I bake rustic, old school bread like brioche, challah, baguette, croissant, focaccia, you name it. Not only does the process help you relieve stress, but that glorious, hypnotic, time-traveling sweet aroma that fills the whole place when that bread rises in the oven and is letting you know it is done, you can eat now.

I remember one night, something was troubling me and keeping me awake. I was sitting in front of the TV, doing nothing, it was late, I was tired but could not sleep. I used to get even angrier by not being able to sleep. Out of an epiphany, or the awakening of the soul in that moment, I decided to bake, I thought ' why not transform this bitch ass stress into something good and positive?'. I went to the kitchen and before I got the elements ready I checked that I had all that was necessary to bake challah bread. And I did, so I rubbed my hands in joy, put some nice music on, and focused on making some nice, golden brown, heavy ancient bread. By midnight, the perfume of yeast, flour, eggs and time filled the house and night with its nostalgic incense. When I took them out of the oven, I could do nothing but stare in delight 3 big braided challah breads over the oven, cooling before I attacked at least one of them. It was a good night, after that I went to sleep happy.

Another craft that disconnects me from the world is writing, I only feel better after writing. Everything you do has a autobiographical factor. So my writing is a lot of me on paper. It does relieve me from all the stress. I spill everything on paper ever since I discovered its art.

I discovered this beautiful art when I once grabbed a small book from my father's shelf. My dad, RIP, was an avid reader; he loved reading and flying away in the pages of great writers. I once wanted to explore that feeling, so I took a small poem book of Pablo Neruda, titled 'Crepusculario'. One specific poem changed everything for me. The tone, the rhythm, the simplicity yet profound aura of it changed my perspective on reading and writing. I said to myself that I wanted to give people the same feeling. I started writing poetry ever since. It is not really what you memorize or understand out of a poem, it is more about what it makes you feel. It's like listening to Vivaldi, or Erik Satie, there are no words, but I'm sure it makes you feel a way that no other song does. I dare you to listen to Vivaldi Summer Presto and feel nothing as it rises like a storm in the air and drags to other times and places.

Writing is a big thing for me, it takes everywhere, to many times, and it relieves me from all stress. I get in the zone; I put some music on, pull out my Moleskine, my pen and get to writing. My whole being goes through the ink onto the blank pages, smearing them with passion, laughter, love, nostalgia, or whatever I am writing about in that moment.

So you see, I do not tell you this out of books, or speeches, this is from experience. But this is my preference, you might like other things, making jewelry, working wood, robotics, programming, painting, as long as it is something you enjoy, do it.

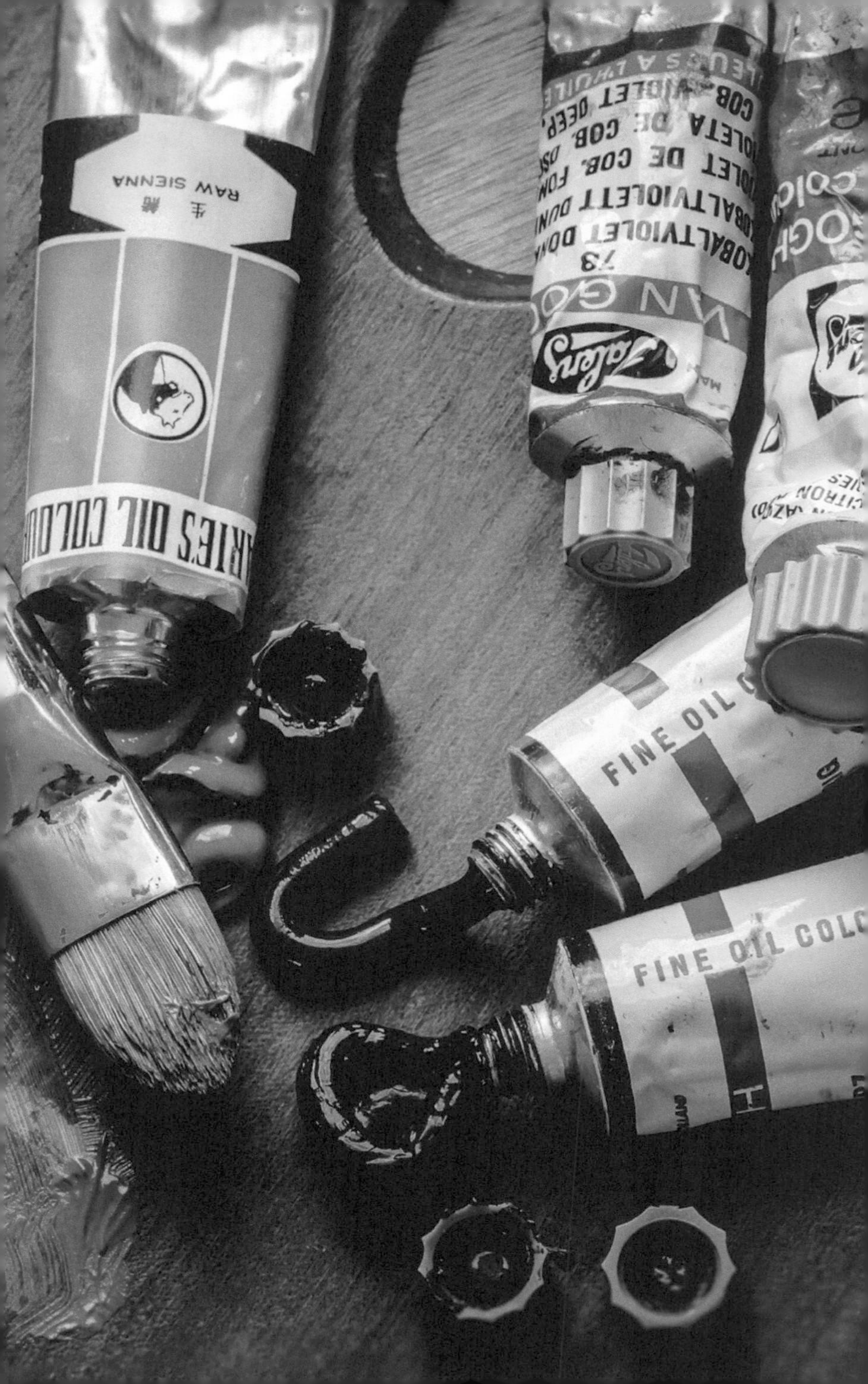
RAW SIENNA
73
FINE OIL
FINE OIL

WHY?

Why? Why are you doing what you do? Asking yourself this question will definitely help you decompress from your daily build-ups. We need to stop for a few seconds, breathe, and ask ourselves why we started this journey, why is it worth going through all of this.

When your answer comes up, trust me, whatever you are going through will seem like nothing, a walk in the park, a small cloud passing by. The struggle is not bigger than your goals.

We do not do things like robots, with no objective, with no purpose. If you ask me why I do what I do, I will answer this: I do it to reach my dreams, to give my wife and kids a better life, comfort, everything they deserve. After this comes up to my mind, it makes my heart warmer, and fills me up with more energy and takes away the stress. How? Focusing on what you want as a goal, considering how grand your destination is, the road is just as enjoyable; you savor whatever comes in the way.

Remember when we were just kids and innocent, and getting dirty didn't matter? When falling from a bike and scraping your knees didn't matter? We would laugh at it, and just get up and keep pedaling until we got where we wanted to go. It was fun; it was adventurous, and simple.

If we fell, we learned what not to do so we don't fall again. There is a saying in Spanish that goes "A veces se gana, otras veces se aprende" and translates to: "sometimes we win, and other times we learn"

So asking yourself why will redirect your course, in case you were wandering, in case you got derailed and take away the sensation of heavy burdens to strengthen you for a great journey to victory. So this will take a few seconds or minutes of your day. It is not complex, it is not something you need a private space to do so, just breathe in, and ask your self: WHY? YOU BADASS SON OF A BITCH, WHY DO YOU DO WHAT YOU DO? The plane will set its course back to its destination, the landing will be safe and all the passengers happy.

LAUGH

Yes, laugh and smile more. Just because we are grown-ups doesn't mean we can't laugh as hard as we used to. We are allowed to laugh, to smile. Shift your tight-ass mindset and laugh at whatever is humorous. Comedians are awesome; I truly admire them. I relate to them and enjoy their stand-ups. They have the ability and virtue of seeing the humor in any situation; they have a great sense of observation and twist every moment to laughter. Isn't this a beautiful thing? Laugh in any given incident. It is about choosing to do so, choosing whether you want to be bitter or laugh at it. It's really up to you.

I had a sad girlfriend once that busted my balls all the time because I found humor in almost anything that happened, while she found everything serious and stressful. I remember one time, we were watching Two and a Half Men, this is a sitcom people, it's sole purpose is to make you laugh, a comedy designed to take away the stress, entertain your mind and have sitting in front of the TV and forget about all the bullshit of that day. I was laughing at the sitcom, and she turns to me with a bitter face and says, " You're so immature, laughing over everything", so I replied politely, "It's called a sense of humor, Google it, and you should purchase some of it". She got pissed obviously, I didn't care, so I just kept watching the show and being 'immature'.

I am not saying laugh at every single thing, all the damn time. But we must loosen up, enjoy life, find the proper humor in situations, and moments. Try to look at life in a different way. The moment you are born you start dying, let that sink in, let that open your eyes, you start oxidizing once you come out of your mother's womb. Is it worth it to be bitter all the time, miss out on laughing and enjoying the short life we have?

What I do is choose what I watch on TV. I do not watch much TV, but when I do, I don't select something just to entertain, just to make noise in the room. This is why I love NETFLIX. I choose comedies and documentaries. Either I laugh or I learn something new, either one of them will surely relieve stress.

I'm home, kids are asleep, gym workout is over and done with, I just showered, lying next to my hot wife, and boom, NETFLIX makes that intro into the living room, I browse through the comedy specials to see which will make me forget about the stress.

To make a point on how laughing helps getting rid of stress, here are some pointers you bitter dumbasses, just in case you think this is a game:

1. Laughter releases a bucketload of happy chemicals that boost immune responses. These chemicals include NK cells (killer cells), endorphins, serotonin, growth hormone, and much more. Not so serious now, huh?
2. Laughing diminishes secretion of cortisol (stress hormone) and epinephrine, enhancing the immune response. Is it clearer?

3. Boosts growth hormone. Beware of people under 5ft!!
4. Endorphins, this is a natural opiate, a natural painkiller, a feel-good hormone. Fuck yeah!!! How about that headache?
5. It can help unblock locked emotions.
6. Stimulates circulation and aids muscle relaxation

Laughing is an all around feel good natural high. Remember when you laughed so much your stomach hurt and you had to run it out so you could stop laughing a bit to breathe; and just after you stopped that hardcore laughter you felt so light, so relaxed and you were just standing there with a dumbass smile on your face and you could fall asleep at that moment of how relaxed you felt. You can still do that; embrace the moment when you do.

DOLCE FAR NIENTE

This means "the sweetness of doing nothing". You probably have heard this in the Julia Roberts movie Eat, Pray, Love. It is not a corny, romantic philosophy. It is part of Italian culture, Italian life.

This is not about becoming lazy or slouching for days. Italians are actually popular for being perfectionists and reflecting quality through their work. They need not tell you, just look into their history, artists, painters, writers, inventors, food, wine, architecture, and scientific discoveries. How much of this has been handed to us by them? Any product that says 'MADE IN ITALY' is synonymous with quality and perfection.

If dolce far niente is part of their culture, it must be nothing less than positive. How? You might ask. It decompresses you to set you back on track.

Savor and drink the moments, enjoy being idle for a change. Not exactly do you have to be lying down and looking at the ceiling. There is a ritual, a design behind being idle. There is a difference between lying in a dark room all day, rather than sitting on a comfortable chair, in front of a window, with the sunlight coming in, some nice music in the background and a cup of coffee or wine. You are still idle, but you are enjoying being idle.

We used to this as young children, but we forgot all about it already. You can reset your mind by doing a few things that keep you in sweet idle stage and clear your mind.

- Turn off your fucking phone. Do you really NEED the phone? Back in the day, nobody had a phone, nobody needed it, and we just called on a landline and spoke for a bit. Turn it off, no social media, no messaging, and no phone ringing. Just disconnect yourself from everything.
- No TV. Spend a day with no TV. Nobody works 7 days a week. We all have a day off or two. Spend one of those days with no TV.
- Hang out, like really hang out with friends or wife, husband, girlfriend, boyfriend, I don't care. Hang out like we used to, leave the phone back home and go for a walk, go to stores, a café and get some coffee, or an early evening cold beer. Sit on a bench and talk shit. Bring some friends over and laugh for a while, eat pizza, forget about diets for one day and enjoy a good fat meal and laugh your ass off with friends or significant other.
- Rest, take a day to truly put yourself to rest, take naps, put some music and relax, don't take off your pajamas for one day and seize the day. Cook on your underwear, sing like no one's watching, let yourself loose and make the day yours.
- Go for a walk. This I enjoy dearly. When it is Sunday after everything has been done I like to take my wife and kids for a walk. When I was single I used to do this a lot, and when my

father was alive, we used to do it regularly. Long walks that clear your head of bad things and fill it up with good ones.

You do not have to do all of these, nor any of these. Pick one and go nuts with it. The whole point is for you, ladies and gentlemen, to have a taste of life, and enjoy the time that we have for ourselves. Don't overthink it, and keep it simple. A good friend of mine and theater director and producer for whom I acted in several dramas, always said to me, "less is more". This ideal fits everything.

GOD

I left this point for the end, is the most sensitive yet profound and powerful. I am not pretending to evangelize anybody nor will I force or persuade you in believing anything you don't agree on.

My spirituality is in a point, not perfect though, that I tolerate whatever faith you practice. Faith, true faith, brings the best out of people. Faith is a belief that good things happen, that there is hope. The other religious people that go to the streets to scream and protest are fanatics. I hate that shit. But, not my problem, I am a Catholic, I believe in Jesus, and whatever you believe in that makes you happy, that brings peace and balance to your life, is good.

Millions of people believe in so many different things and that is as good. I have friends from many religions and we hang out and get along perfectly.

Nevertheless, the point is, having a faith, believing in something higher than all human existence brings balance, brings hope and calms us down. Whatever you believe in, treasure it, and let that be your shelter.

Any religion, scripture, and spiritual congregation can only be positive; it goes beyond any hardship.

If we adhere to the spiritual values and the ethics that it teaches us, we can't go wrong. Holding on to faith will help us focus; will stabilize your thoughts and fears, including your stress.

There have been many studies made on how faith is linked to mental health. All of them have shown that faith, religion, spirituality, whatever you want to call it, has a positive outcome on mental health. The more religious and spiritual you are, the better your mental health is. Start praying brothers and sisters, and keep your hopes up. It only gets better.

When you have strong bonds with a religion, you study it and realize how many have gone through so my tough times, keeping their faith to the end, seeing how this faith has helped them rise up stronger than before.

Speaking for myself, I used to be a mess, I was an ignorant adolescent that lost his father and blamed everything on that, blamed everything on everybody, angry all the time, and hating all the time. Until I went back to basics, went back home to God. In the most obscure time I reached out blindly to God. I immediately felt better, warm, and full of hope. I realize that I am not the only one going through such difficult times, I am not the first or last that will experience such sadness, such a loss. Every one has a story that marks them, but how you get a grip of it and let it change you is what makes the difference. So I let God change me for the better, I let Him humble me, and every day since, I speak to him as I am, and put everything on His hands while I work down here with mine to make things happen.